Wildflowers Of The American West

Wildflowers Of The American West

*A Photographic Celebration of
Nature's Beauty*

Written by Rose Houk
Designed by McQuiston & Daughter

Chronicle Books, San Francisco

To Michael

There are several people who helped make this book a reality. I have only mere words to show my gratitude. Consultant Claudia Rector's knowledge about the flowers and things botanical were indispensable in writing this book. Above that, though, she more than once provided me with a warm fire and always responded with boundless enthusiasm. She has been a continuing source of inspiration.

Frankie Wright knew all the right things to say at the right time. To her I owe only what an author can owe to a good editor. To Don and Debra McQuiston my thanks for the opportunity to do this book. Their design talents and love for the subject show through in every page of the book. Making a book requires a great amount of trust among many people. There was never a question in my mind that they would produce their usual best.
—ROSE HOUK

Photographers who direct their attention to wildflowers are surely patient souls—patient with Nature's unpredictable calendar, with changing light and sudden breezes. For their added patience with our very predictable calendar, we thank the exceptional photographers who have contributed to this book. Their artistry celebrates a truly artful subject.

Michael Eagleton deserves special thanks for his exquisite renderings of prairie wildflowers. These delicate and masterful paintings carry forth a tradition flowers have inspired for ages.

We are grateful to Jack Jensen and David Barich for their confidence in this project and to the many others at Chronicle Books for their continued support.
—McQUISTON & DAUGHTER

Produced and designed by McQuiston & Daughter, Del Mar, California; Edited by Frankie Wright; Botanical consultation and review by Claudia Dean Rector; Mechanical production by Curt Boyer; Composition by Thompson Type; Printed in Japan by Dai Nippon Printing Co., through Interprint, San Francisco

Library of Congress Cataloging in Publication Data:
Houk, Rose, 1950-
    Wildflowers of the American West.
    Bibliography: p.106
    Includes index.
    1. Wildflowers—West (U.S.) 2. Wild flowers—West (U.S.)— Pictorial works.   I. Title.
QK133.H68   1987   582.13'0978   87-782
ISBN 0-87701-424-8
ISBN 0-87701-435-3 (pbk.)
10 9 8 7 6 5 4 3 2 1

Distributed in Canada by Raincoast Books
112 East Third Avenue
Vancouver, British Columbia V5T 1C8

Chronicle Books, One Hallidie Plaza
San Francisco, California 94102

Photo Credits
Front cover: Pink monkeyflower and lupine
Back cover: Indian paintbrush by Pat O'Hara
Frontispiece: Sego or mariposa lily by Jeff Gnass
Title page: Paintbrush by William Neill
Contents page: Woolly lasthenia and iris by Larry Ulrich

Contents

W e are fortunate to be living now. Not so long ago there were no flowers in the world, a dreadful thought to entertain. In the wink of an eye in geologic time, flowers colonized land in a takeover that was the Boston Tea Party of evolution.

"Flowers changed the face of the planet. Without them, the world we know—even man himself—would never have existed." Paleontologist Loren Eiseley wrote this and explained. Flowers evolved during the age of reptiles, some 120 million years ago. At the time, dinosaurs plodded across the swampy land, eating one another on occasion, but by and large the world was green and somnolent by our standards. Near the end of that age, flowering plants made their sudden entrance. They took advantage of all sorts of new opportunities. They diversified, and with their unmatched versatility became roaring successes. By providing food for warm-blooded creatures like ourselves, flowers changed the patterns of life on the earth.

Flowering plants, or angiosperms, had a significant invention, the encased seed, that pines and spruces did not possess. The word angiosperm means "encased seed." Within the flower's ovary the seed could be protected in a self-contained life support system, enhancing chances for its survival. With the evolution of flowers, plants came up with a host of new pollination schemes. They had at their disposal not only wind and water, and better ways to use them, but also animals. Insects, birds, bats, and even nonflying mammals were attracted to their bright colors and scents. Flowers offered pollen and nectar as food, and animals reciprocated by aiding cross-pollination of the flowers.

Paintbrush and larkspur

(opposite page) by Larry Ulrich,

shooting star (far right)

by Tom and Pat Leeson

Animal pollinators have coevolved with flowers in complex relationships that are mutually beneficial. In the course of obtaining food, pollinators rub against pollen-bearing anthers on one flower. On a visit to the next flower, they leave the golden dust on the sticky pistils. From the pollen a tube grows down the pistil to the ovule, the seed-to-be. The sperm nucleus, which contains the genetic material of the male parent, travels down that tube. When it unites with the ovule, fertilization occurs and a new seed is formed.

Over millions of years these pollinators have become matched with the showy parts and scents of certain flowers. Deep-throated white flowers like datura generally open at night when moths are making their rounds. Nocturnal insects are attracted to the white blooms visible in the dark. Red flowers, especially pendant ones, invite daytime pollinators like hummingbirds. Hummers can see red and use their long beaks and tongues to dip into trumpet-shaped flowers. The compound flowers of daisies have "display" petals to attract pollinators to the center of the flower.

Some flowers offer landing platforms on which insects can alight; others lead their pollinators in by visual and tactile lines called nectar- or honey-guides. Not all of these lines are visible to us, but insects and birds, which can see ultraviolet wavelengths, can detect them easily. Chutes and windows lure pollinators too. Some flowers actually close their petals to trap insects, forcing them to contact pollen as they struggle to exit.

Pollinators must also be on time. Flowers have intricate daily and seasonal rhythms that control movement, scent, nectar production, and blooming period. So precise are these rhythms that some people set their watches by flowers. Four o'clocks are so named for opening at that hour in the afternoon.

These imperfectly understood rhythms appear to be controlled by hormones released from leaves and by alterations in cell membranes. In some cases, too, extremely fine changes in temperature, light, or humidity affect flowering. Sensitive snow gentians, for example, close when a cloud passes overhead and reopen with the sunshine.

Besides acting as timepieces, flowers have earned our respect for many other reasons. For us they are sources of food, medicines, dyes, oils, spices, fibers, and perfumes. Plains pioneers even burned the stalks of sunflowers as fuel. Flowers fill aesthetic and emotional needs as well, acting as tokens of love, sympathy, happiness, and goodwill. They symbolize months, seasons, and years, and in the Victorian "language of flowers" each one corresponded to a virtue or a vice.

As we get to know flowers, they become our friends. And like friends, we want to know their names. An entire lexicon of picturesque vernacular names surrounds the flowering world, their sources as ingenious as the flowers themselves. Common names come from the flowers' discoverers, myths and folklore, supposed healing properties, foreign languages, and the colors, shapes, and smells of flowers, just to name a few.

There's sneezeweed and cankerwort, bee balm and boneset, aster and anemone, adder's-tongue and lady's slipper. Chinook Indians of the Northwest gave us camas, their word for bulb. From the Spaniards, we have mariposa, the butterfly lily. The red clintonia, a lily of the redwood forests, honors, oddly enough, DeWitt Clinton, a former governor of New York. Henry David Thoreau, incidentally, complained that canals and railroads, not flowers, should be named after politicians. (In truth, the good governor botanized in his spare time and was a naturalist of some repute.)

The beautiful columbines that grow in our western mountains struck a poetic chord. Their name is from the Latin *columba*, or dove, because the flowers were thought to resemble a circle of doves. Another beauty that grows in secluded places, the calypso orchid, was named for the sea nymph Calypso, "she who conceals." From the Hindu *Dhatura* comes the name for the flower we call datura, sacred to many North American Indians.

Charming and memorable though they may be, common names can lead us astray. Arising willy-nilly, with little consistency in different parts of the country, they can often confuse.

Alas, we must inevitably turn to the tongue-twisting Latin and Greek for true guidance down this prickly path. In the botanical world, scientific names are the signposts to heed. They're not so bad, actually, once you become accustomed to pronouncing them. They can tell us a great deal more about a flower, add to a fond relationship with it, and deciphering them, we often learn that they are the true sources of the popular names.

8

In the eighteenth century Carolus Linnaeus devised the scientific nomenclature of the plant world. In the Linnaean system, the accepted plant name consists of two words, either in Latin or Greek. The first word, capitalized, is the genus; the second is the species. Linnaeus also revolutionized his discipline by creating a classification system that botanists today still follow. It has been said that "God created, Linnaeus ordered."

Linnaeus used the stamens and pistils of flowers—the reproductive parts of the plant—as the basis for the classes, stirring up a hornet's nest with his controversial notion that the "lower" kingdom of plants reproduced sexually. His mind was one of "gross prurience," snorted one righteous reverend. Other influential people, however, believed that Linnaeus's system was the work of genius, and before long he was receiving the highest honors of the European scientific world.

Scientists have their differences, of course, and to avoid creating any additional confusion, we have selected one source as our primary authority for scientific names: *The Audubon Society Field Guide to North American Wildflowers* by Richard Spellenberg. We have stayed with this nomenclature in almost all cases. We have also made constant reference to the comprehensive multivolume work by Harold William Rickett, *Wild Flowers of the United States*. 🌱

This book is intended, through illustrations and words, to share the beauty of wildflowers. Our first criterion for inclusion was that the flower be native to the western United States. Beyond this, flowers were selected based on their conspicuousness along road or trail.

We have tried to include those that are noticeable in their abundance or by their uniqueness. In some cases we bowed to a flower's sheer beauty, or, if it must be confessed, to personal favorites. Trees, shrubs, and vines were omitted, and only herbaceous flowering plants are featured. The only exception is in the desert section, which did not seem complete without a cactus or two.

Somewhat arbitrarily, for there are many ways to do this, the book is organized into four sections: coast, desert, mountain, and prairie. Coast includes the beaches and dunes along the Pacific Ocean, the Coast Ranges that rise from the shore, the Great Valley of California, and the foothills of the Sierra Nevada. Desert encompasses the four major North American deserts of the United States—the Sonoran, Chihuahuan, Mohave, and Great Basin. By mountains, we mean those high, glaciated ranges of the West, primarily the Rocky Mountains, Sierra Nevada, Cascades, and Olympic Mountains. This section also includes flowers found in the highest elevations on the mountain islands and high plateaus of the Southwest. Prairie is limited primarily to the Great Plains, from the one hundredth meridian west to the foothills of the Rockies.

Wildflowers frequently fail to obey these boundaries. Though some are quite specific in their habitat preferences, others are much more cosmopolitan. Paintbrushes, lupines, and poppies, for instance, grow in more than one of our four divisions. Again, sometimes arbitrarily, we were forced to choose one section in which to show them in this book.

We have not intended to provide a field guide for identifying wildflowers. Many excellent guides are in print and we urge you to turn to them for details on a specific flower during your sojourns in the field. Instead, we wish to share some of the interesting stories behind their names, facts about their biology, and folklore about medicinal uses. Any mention of a plant's historic use as medicine or as food is *not* to be taken as an endorsement that such use is beneficial or even safe.

Consistent with the aim of this book—appreciation of wildflowers—a word about collecting flowers is appropriate. Points of view vary widely on this subject, and it is difficult to make dogmatic statements. Most states now have laws that protect certain species of plants, but they are not all-encompassing. National parks and monuments prohibit the collection of any material within their borders. For plants not legally protected, however, a personal ethic toward the land must govern. Never dig up a plant's root; where they are abundant, annual flowers can be gathered if enough are left to produce seed for another year. If in doubt about a plant's status, always err on the side of conservatism. For sources of wildflower seeds, inquire of native plant societies and local nurseries in your area. Tempting though it may be to take just one, a flower is always more beautiful in its home than ours. 🌱

9

Our country, it seems, has always been on a mad rush to the West Coast. The coast has lured people like so many schools of fish. No sooner had they settled the eastern seaboard than they were off in wagons, on horses, by ship, or by rail, drugged with the thought of reaching the golden shores of the Pacific.

Around 1880, after the first great emigration of the '40s, boosters geared up to snag more settlers. They sang the praises of the promised land: "Whoever asks where Los Angeles is, to him I shall say: across a desert without wearying, beyond a mountain without climbing . . . where the flowers catch fire with beauty. . . ." B. F. Taylor wrote these words in *Between the Gates*. He continued with promises of pomegranates, bananas, chestnuts, lemons, and almonds growing in profusion in the Land of Lotus, the Cornucopia of the World.

If they survived the Great Basin desert and the Sierra Nevada, the newcomers did indeed find a seductive land on the edge of the continent. Those who veered north, though, for Oregon and Washington, found something entirely different than did those who stayed on the California trail.

For 1,700 miles the coast extends from Washington's Olympic Peninsula to Baja California. This great expanse takes in wave-pounded cliffs, calm bays and lagoons, ocean beaches, low mountains, rivers, and rolling hills. Dense rainforest, towering redwoods, scrubby chaparral, and grasses cover the land. The Coast Ranges, a series of unconnected hills and mountains, abruptly

Lupine (opposite page)

and giant trillium (far right)

by Larry Ulrich

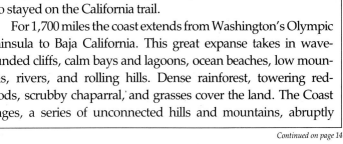

Continued on page 14

William Neill

O W L ' S C L O V E R

Orthocarpus spp.

The velvety clusters of soft rose and white of owl's clover make a breathtaking display interspersed on grassy hillsides with blue lupine and gold poppies.

A closer look at this flower reveals a white or yellow three-lobed pouch with an inflated lower lip and a long hooked beak arching over the top, architecture that marks it as a member of the snapdragon family.

Within the coastal region owl's clover blooms from March to May in southern California, inland to the San Joaquin Valley, and over to the deserts of western Arizona. Mostly it is an aficionado of pastures and grasslands, putting on its best shows after a wet winter.

The Spanish call it *escobita*, or little broom, for its resemblance to a whiskbroom. The source of the English common name is some-what obscure. But if you use your imagination, you might be able to see the flower heads peering from the bracts like an owl from a tree.

jut up from the shore. Though they average only 2,000 to 4,000 feet in elevation, their sudden rise from the continent's edge lends great relief to the terrain. On the eastern side of the Coast Ranges, grassy hills roll down to the Great Valley of California, almost to sea level again. Beyond the Great Valley stretches the Sierra Nevada, the barrier between the temperate coast and dry deserts on the far side.

Even during June, the driest month, it rains in the forests of the Olympic Peninsula. This region receives the continent's heaviest precipitation—nearly 140 inches each year. Farther south, on the central coast of California, the climate is often described as Mediterranean. By the time the Mexican border is reached, south of San Diego, rainfall has dropped to ten inches annually, qualifying the area as desert.

The signs of dryness begin to reveal themselves south of Monterey Bay, as verdant forests give way to low-growing scrub and grasses, golden brown for half the year. The landforms, too, begin to smooth out, the surf becomes lazier, and the hills less steep.

Despite these extremes, overall the Pacific Coast boasts one of the most comfortable, consistent climates anywhere. The great tempering influence is the Pacific Ocean, its currents and winds bringing cool fresh sea breezes onshore in summer and soggy storms in winter. All along the coast, there are basically two seasons—wet and dry. Summers, from May through October, are dry. Winters, from November to May, are wet.

In 1579, while anchored north of San Francisco, Sir Francis Drake despaired of the "most vile, thicke and stinking fogges," that had detained him. As Drake and others quickly learned, fog is a constant presence on the coast, swathing forests and hills in soft pillows of grey and white. Robert Louis Stevenson wrote of a bank of white fog that "swallowed a piece of mountain at a gulp." Born over the ocean, fogs waft into shore, pushed by a high pressure system and pulled by land-based low pressures. In summer, the process reverses itself, with fog drifting from the land and eventually dissipating over the ocean.

The fog region and the coastal redwood belt are nearly identical. From the Coast Range in Oregon to canyons below Monterey, redwoods thrive in the deep fertile soils of the river valleys. Among the earth's oldest and tallest living organisms, they owe their existence to the moisture-laden fogs, which carry astonishing amounts of water in the form of vapor. As the vapor condenses it bathes the redwoods, nourishing them to their 300-foot heights.

In the ethereal light of the redwood forest grow luxurious masses of ferns, violas, trilliums, fritillaries, and a bad-smelling flower that has earned the unseemly name of fetid adder's-tongue. The small flowers of redwood sorrel carpet the spongy floor. Dainty sugar scoops and fringe cups lend sharp contrast to the giant trees towering above them.

Over the years, redwoods have inspired both conservationists and lumbermen. But for coastal settlers, oak woodlands were their favored townsites. As Peter Steinhart has written, "There is about the oaks a feeling of ease and patient endurance that was much a part of the California past." Franciscan missionaries followed the oak-wooded valleys north, hanging mission bells from the trees' gnarled limbs. Some of these oaks are part of a fascinating coastal plant community known as chaparral. Where rainfall averages between ten and twenty inches a year, chaparral smothers lower mountain slopes and foothills from south of San Francisco into Baja. The scrub oak that the Spanish vaqueros called *chaparro* inspired its name. Besides the oaks, chaparral is made up of about a dozen shrubs, including wild lilac and red-barked manzanita. These leathery-leaved, deep-rooted shrubs grow in nearly impenetrable thickets, protecting the soil from erosion.

In chaparral country, "spring" begins in November, when welcome rains sop the tinder-dry hillsides. After a burst of green, wildflowers begin to run rampant. Phacelia, lupines, snapdragons, poppies, and penstemons cloak the hillsides. The centaury, or canchalagua, a member of the family that includes gentians, grows alongside suncups, star lilies, and blue dicks.

California's Great Valley is one of the few places in the world with ecosystems called vernal pools. Each spring the water in these remnant glacial lakes evaporates. Apparently the combination of Mediterranean climate and underlying dense clay makes these dried pools excellent wildflower habitat. Some support more than a hundred species, bellflowers, goldfields, monkeyflowers, and meadowfoam among them. John Muir tells us of the Great Valley's former glory. In March, April, and May the valley "was one smooth, continuous bed of honey-bloom," and for its four-hundred-mile length "your foot would press about a hundred flowers at every step."

California was shown on early maps as an island. In many ways the first cartographers were right, at least as far as the state's plant life is concerned. A good deal of California's flora have developed in isolation from the rest of the country, creating many distinctive members. Unique to California, the cypresses and the Monterey, bishop, and Torrey pines have become symbols of the coast. Growing along beach strands and the seaward, fog-dampened slopes, they are exposed to ocean salt spray and battering winds. The effects are evident in their size and shape—small and gnarled, with the seaward side bare of branches. Perhaps some plants will grow only where they can hear the sound of the waves, as people in the tropics say of their coconut palm.

Smaller shore and beach plants share with plants of other regions several adaptations to dry, salty conditions. The common ice plant and sea fig, both introduced along the coast, have succulent forms that allow them to tolerate the high concentration of salts from ocean mists. Like desert plants, beach and shore species have developed fleshy leaves in which they can store the hard-won water. Among the shifting dunes, seaside daisies, sea asters, and sand verbenas grow compactly and close to the ground as a defense against wind.

Though still part of the "earth's most magnificent coast," the Pacific Northwest is far lonelier, wilder, and more mysterious than its southern counterpart. As one travels northward up the coast, the flavor changes drastically. Place names here have a new sound:

Siskiyou, Neskowin, Tillamook, and Hoquiam, the names given by the region's first people. The surf and the rivers take on a strength and ferocity not known to the south. Onshore, the land is overwhelmingly ruled by trees.

A trio of stately trees lives in the Northwest forests—Sitka spruce, western hemlock, and western red cedar. The biggest Sitka spruce are found right down to the Pacific shore on the Olympic Peninsula. They cling to the tidelands and mouths of streams along the coast south to Mendocino. Western hemlock is the most abundant tree of the Pacific coastal forest. It thrives on the moisture of lowlands and seaward slopes, and like Sitka spruce, takes nicely to dense shade. The third tree, western red cedar, is often called the "canoe cedar" for its use by both coast Indians and by Lewis and Clark, who built five dugout canoes from red cedar and floated down the Columbia River to the ocean.

These three giants form the top story of the rainforest. Beneath them are a layer of deciduous trees and a ground story of berry bushes, mosses, ferns, and flowers. Early spring bloomers include the pioneer violet, trillium, and salmonberry. By May the oxalis, foamflower, and woodnymph blossom among the pyrolas and starflowers. Though a few, like oxalis and trillium, tolerate the shade, others need the sunlight of meadows and clearings.

On the wild, rock-bound beaches of the Northwest coast the salt spray is literally diluted by the prodigious rains, and flowers like the pearly everlasting can be found blooming. Beyond the seascape the skunk cabbage of swales and swamps, dogtooth violets of open woods, and coral roots of deep forests mark this botanically rich and distinct region.

The coast, then, with its extremes of diversity, is actually a microcosm of the entire western United States. Deserts, grasslands, forests, mountains, they are all here. There is something for everyone, which perhaps has always been its greatest lure. 🐚

Larry Ulrich

T R I L L I U M

Trillium spp.

*A*ll parts of the trillium come in threes: leaves, sepals, petals, styles, and the reddish berry. Not surprisingly the name comes from the Latin *triplum*, for three. Trillium is one of the earliest spring bloomers, showing up along streams and in woods from February to June.

The flowers, ranging from pure white to pinkish to rich maroon, are carried atop a single stout stem and are held in the hand of three broad leaves. The large leaves, sometimes mottled, reminded Mary Elizabeth Parsons of "decorated pieces of china that have been several times through the kiln."

Those who know the trillium from the coast and mountains of the West have a charming name for it—the wake robin, because it shows up with the early bird. Appalachian mountain folk know it not only as wake robin but by an entire litany of intriguing common names: bathwort, birthroot, daffydown-dilly, dishcloth, nosebleed, stinking Benjamin, and true love. The root of trillium reportedly was used by Indian women to ease the pain of childbirth, hence the explanation for the name birthroot. We can only speculate about the meanings behind dishcloth, nosebleed, or true love.

Larry Ulrich

I R I S

Iris spp.

Iris, the winged messenger of the gods, was the rainbow, and for her colorful cloak the iris flower was named. From delicate amethyst, the colors of iris vary to cream and yellow. The darker pen-and-ink lines etched on the petals guide bees to the flower's pollen.

Several species of irises grow in the West, preferring wet places for the most part. Those that grow along the coast include, among others, the ground and tough-leaved iris. One, the Douglas iris, is named for Scottish botanist David Douglas, who explored extensively in the Northwest during the mid-1800s. *Iris missouriensis*, found east of the Cascade Range, was discovered by a famous early botanist, Thomas Nuttall. He found it near the headwaters of the Missouri River, hence its species name.

The grasslike leaves, typical of irises, have an interesting habit that Linnaeus termed "equitant." Older leaves fold lengthwise around younger leaves, "like one astride a horse's back."

Ancient Greeks valued the iris for its catholic medicinal properties: it cured "spleens," coughs, bruises, fits, dropsy, snakebites, and anger. Later, people believed that beads of the root worn as a necklace served the worthwhile function of removing the smell of liquor, garlic, and tobacco. Orrisroot, used in perfumes, comes from the rootstock of several species.

Larry Ulrich

SEASIDE DAISY

Erigeron spp.

Always within sound of the surf, the cheery flowers of the seaside daisy bloom from April to August on coastal bluffs, beaches, and old dunes. Unlike others of its kind, this daisy dons a habit that lets it live near the coast—fleshy, hairy leaves that protect against drying wind and salt spray.

The violet "petals" are actually minute flowers, and this daisy may have as many as a hundred such ray flowers surrounding the center disk of yellow. The center too is composed of many individual flowers or florets, giving us a clue to its family affiliation. Daisies, along with asters, fleabanes, dandelions, and a number of familiar flowers, are composites. The particular genus, *Erigeron*, is recognized by several features, including bracts around the flower head that are all about the same size.

The word daisy is a corruption of "day's eye," given to an English daisy that closed at night and opened at dawn. In Welsh it was Llygad y Dydd, or Eye of the Day. Contemplation of a daisy led John Bartram to establish America's first botanic garden, and Robert Burns, the Scottish poet and farmer, once wrote a verse to the daisy in repentance for taking its life by the plow.

Daisies are innocence, and with buttercups and dandelions, are the gold and white symbols of childhood.

Larry Ulrich, *(opposite page)* Jeff Gnass

PITCHER PLANT & TIGER LILY

Darlingtonia californica & Lilium spp.

eaves of the California pitcher plant (*facing page*) hold its true fascination. Highly modified, several leaves on each plant are long inflated tubes that curve at their top into a hood with an opening. From the hood grow two appendages whose nectar attracts insects. Once on the opening of the "pitcher," insects slide down inside the slippery hood and soon find themselves in a pool at the bottom, with no way out. Slowly, bacteria in the fluid decompose the insects, providing nutrients for the plant.

All members of the pitcher plant family are carnivorous, a feature that makes some humans squirm. Words often used to describe them are "macabre," "diabolical," or "unnatural." Their uniqueness has made them objects of collectors for many years, a practice that threatens their survival.

Several lilies of the West Coast are called tiger lily (*this page*) and strongly resemble one another: Columbia, Humboldt's, Sierra, and leopard or panther, among them. They flower prolifically in the summer months in thickets and open forests, on hillsides, and in moist places. As with all lilies, they grow from a scaly bulbous root.

An old legend tells that after a rain the lilies of the Caucasus would change color, sometimes to red, sometimes to yellow. Maidens could tell their fortunes from them: if a bud opened yellow they suspected their lovers of unfaithfulness; if it was red, they knew them to be true. But what of the orange varieties? Our fair maidens would be sorely confused, we fear.

2   4

Tom and Pat Leeson

S K U N K   C A B B A G E

Lysichitum spp.

A "firstling," skunk cabbage pokes up early through the swampish waters or the duff of the forest floor. Nothing is more typical of winter's end in the wet western forests than its appearance. Crowded in a thick swamp, they looked to botanist Leslie Haskin like "fairy boatmen in coats of gold who have gathered to honor the coming of spring with a water fete."

Skunk cabbage is a member of the arum family, a collection of unusual plants mostly of tropical persuasion. Jack-in-the-pulpit of the eastern forests and wild calla lily are close relations. On skunk cabbage a waxy yellow or cream-colored spathe, open on one side, covers the flowers like a hood. Inside is a spadix, or fleshy column, bearing hundreds of minute yellow flowers. The sleek green leaves, similar to those on banana trees, grow up to five feet long.

The unpleasant odor of the bruised plant has given weight to the name skunk cabbage. Despite this, people have not been deterred in finding a number of uses for it. The peppery sap has been said to help cases of ringworm and rheumatism. The roots, also peppery, can be cooked and eaten, as can the young greens. Boiling or cooking these parts removes the stinging acridness caused by calcium oxalate.

Bears covet all parts of the plant and will ravage an area digging it out.

Larry Ulrich

R E D W O O D   S O R R E L

Oxalis oregana

n cool glades of the coast redwood forests this plant lays itself out in large patches. Solitary white to pink flowers, barely an inch, are poised amid a welter of cloverlike leaves.

The leaves of this wood sorrel, perhaps more than the flower, are most notable. They close at night, and during the daytime constantly adjust themselves to the muted light filtering through the lacy foliage of the great trees. Their whitish centers caused Mary Elizabeth Parsons to muse in *The Wild Flowers of California*: "If the goddess Nanna in passing left the print of her pretty fingers upon the clover, perhaps some wood-nymph may have touched the leaves of this charming plant."

The heart-shaped leaves of wood sorrel led early herbalists to apply the "doctrine of signatures." If certain plants resembled a part of the body, then they must logically aid in curing any ailment afflicting that part. Hence, sorrel leaves were a cordial, or heart restorative. In Europe the wood sorrel was called hallelujah, because it bloomed at Easter when the chorus was sung. Many believe the three-part leaves were the original shamrock, which gave St. Patrick the power to drive the snakes from Ireland and which people wear on March 17 to honor the saint.

Larry Ulrich

BUNCHBERRY

Cornus canadensis

A dogwood tree in miniature is the bunchberry or dwarf cornel. Like the eastern and southern trees that bloom so profusely in spring, this is a member of the dogwood family, but it is a low creeping herb rather than a tree. A whorl of green leaves forms a pillow for the white bracts, that are, coincidentally, not the flower. A hand lens is almost necessary to examine the tiny greenish flowers that cluster in the center of the bracts.

Bunchberry, crackerberry, or puddingberry are common names that arise from the bright red berries. They develop from the flowers, also in tight clusters. Ruffed grouse and other birds nibble their "insipid" flesh, and New Englanders used them in their plum duff, hence puddingberry.

From May or June to July or August the bunchberry blooms in moist cool woods in the coastal mountains, and at least one botanist says they are at their best in open woods in the Cascades.

The dogwood speaks of durability. The genus name, *Cornus,* refers to its exceedingly hard wood. In the Middle Ages, it is reported, butchers used the wood for skewers. And dogwood tea was the prescription for a colicky baby.

3 0

BLUE DICK

Brodiaea pulchella

The blue to violet flowers of this perennial are in a head on naked stalks. Their lily traits are apparent in the six petal-like parts and six stamens, grasslike leaves, and underground corm. Blooming from February or March into May, blue dicks are common on plains and grasslands in most of California west of the Sierras, and into Oregon.

The blue dick is one of some forty species of *Brodiaea* that grow in western North America and South America. Several species are similar, sharing the characteristic naked stalk, hyacinth-like flowers, and narrow leaves. They range from pink and red, to blue and violet flowers. Some are yellow or white.

One brodiaea, Ithuriel's spear, was named for an angel who found Satan in the form of a toad trying to tempt Eve. Ithuriel touched the devil with his spear and changed him into his real personage. Yet another species was called "ookow" by Indians. The sweet bulbs, when cooked, filled a need for bread and potatoes. Grassnut, cluster lily, and wild hyacinth are other common names. The name brodiaea is for a Scottish botanist, J. J. Brodie.

Expressing concern about encroaching development along California's Big Sur coast, Mary Wentworth Owings asks in the book *Not Man Apart*, "But where, in all this, would the brodeia hills of childhood be? Where in the years to come would we find the slopes covered by blooms reflecting the sky in their petals?"

32

Larry Ulrich

CALIFORNIA POPPY

Eschscholtzia californica

Johann Friedrich Eschscholtz was honored by having his name attached to this exemplary flower. He was a Russian naturalist and surgeon with Kotzebue's *Rurik* expedition to California in 1816. But nearly everywhere it is simply the California poppy, the flower that lights up the coastal hills and valleys and says "California" to all who know it.

Indeed, early Spanish mariners, seeing hillsides cloaked in goldish-orange, were moved to call the area "the land of fire." Tradition has it that a mesa near Pasadena shone so brightly with the poppies' flaming orange that the hill served as a beacon to ships. The Spaniards, in their beautiful language, called the flower *copa de oro*, "cup of gold."

California poppies "sleep" at night and on cloudy or foggy days. They close their fan-shaped petals and open only in full sun. The petals awake with a stretch, breaking away the budlike calyx that contains them. The flower's spicy fragrance invites beetles, its main pollinator.

Either annual or perennial, the poppy assumes various forms depending upon where it grows. Along coastal dunes it withstands ocean breezes by becoming a compact annual; inland it is a larger perennial.

A pink rim at the base of the ovary, conspicuous when the petals fall off, distinguishes this species from others that resemble it.

W ater is the great equalizer. Nearly anyone who has tried to define desert eventually comes around to that one fundamental conclusion. The great paradox of a desert is that with less water than anywhere else on earth, life can and does exist, and at times flourishes.

In certain years, mainly in the spring, deserts in the West put on one of the best wildflower shows in the world. Lupines and lilies and daisies and marigolds stage riots of color on the hillsides. Desert observer John Van Dyke saw one of these shows and gave this review: "Sometimes beds of these flowers extend for miles, spreading in variegated sweeps of color, apparently undulating like a brilliant carpet swayed by the wind."

How is this paradox explained? Not unexpectedly, the answer rests with moisture. Years may pass when not enough rain falls to stimulate plant growth. But when a good dousing does come in early winter or midsummer, a wildflower extravaganza can be anticipated.

The "ephemerals" are the least bashful in taking advantage of these precious rains. Ephemerals, or short-season annuals, are plants that seem to disappear nearly as quickly as they appeared; they germinate, bloom, and go to seed within five or six weeks. Naturalist Ruth Kirk believes that "If a prize could be awarded for recognizing opportunity and turning it to good account, these plants should be the recipients." Poppies, owl's clover, and desert dandelions, among others, fall into this category, brightening the desert floor in those special years of generous rainfall.

Poppies and owl's clover

with cholla cactus (opposite page)

by David Muench, poppies

(far right) by Paul Johnson

Continued on page 38

FOUR O'CLOCK

Mirabilis spp.

W onderful, marvelous." These are the words botanists thought best described this bright flower, and so they applied the Latin word *Mirabilis* to the genus. The Spanish also give their word for marvelous, *maravilla*, to the four o'clock.

The desert species sports a host of purple-pink blossoms on a low mound of dark green leaves. From April to September the large flowers of this perennial grace open sandy or rocky areas, mesas, and hills—from low deserts into pinyon-juniper forests.

The common name comes from its habit of opening late in the afternoon, making four o'clocks choice plants to include in a floral clock. A favorite of gardeners is the South American version, the common four o'clock or marvel-of-Peru.

Along with evening primroses, four o'clock "will keep the vigils of the night," believed Mary Elizabeth Parsons. She might have added that they will also furnish nectar for the hawkmoth that visits in the evening.

Members of the four o'clock family lack petals and instead have colored sepals that look and act like petals.

What the sensitive seeds of ephemerals are waiting for, during their dormancy, is just the right amount and kind of rain, at the right time. A gentle, not necessarily torrential, downpour of even a half-inch will do the trick. But it must be rain, and it must come down through the soil, rather than up from underlying layers, to dissolve the chemical barrier that many seeds contain. These coatings are so resistant that even a soaking in acid or corrosives does not damage the embryo inside the seed.

Temperature is another critical element in germination of these ephemerals. In the Sonoran Desert of southern Arizona, at least, spring annuals find a germination temperature of 60 to 65 degrees Fahrenheit optimum. Summer annuals, those that respond to the monsoons of July and August, need higher temperatures, about 80 to 90 degrees. After the first heavy rain in July, the summer annuals appear and enjoy a somewhat longer season than their spring counterparts.

Annuals are quintessential drought escapers, and thus enjoy great success in deserts. Rather than wasting energy sending up leaves and stems during dry times, they simply live as seeds in the ground until conditions are right for them to grow and flower.

Perennials, on the other hand, must somehow find ways to endure or avoid the heat and dryness. Members of the cactus clan are experts at this. These spine-covered succulents store water in fleshy pads and stems, vegetable reservoirs that carry them through hard times. When they do bloom, in bright magentas, reds, yellows, and oranges, the flowers adorn them like faceted jewels. Being so well-adapted to desert conditions, cacti can bloom during much of the desert year; usually, though, they wait until after the winter rains. Some bloom for only one day, others last six months. Night-blooming cereus, the queen of the night, holds within its gargantuan, turniplike root enough water to permit the tender white blossoms to open even in the driest part of summer.

Shrubs like creosote bush, blackbrush, saltbush, and sagebrush account for a great deal of desert vegetation. They too must persist in whatever punishment the desert metes out. They lose leaves, extend roots, and hide their pores to lessen the loss of precious water to the dry air. They keep their distance from one another, lending the distinct feeling of an oriental garden to the vast shrub-covered plains and valleys.

Though plants are innocent of such things, we humans often turn to numbers to tell us what is really happening in nature. Desert dwellers, understandably, are often preoccupied with rainfall patterns and statistics, numbers that can instill a false sense of security and certainty. In October 1983 residents of Tucson, Arizona learned that those patterns and statistics are not always worth much. In a single weekend the city received almost seven inches of rain, or half its average annual rainfall. Saturday kayakers played on fifteen-foot waves on the Rillito River, a normally dry wash, while pieces of condominiums sailed past them. Bridges washed out, and for that weekend it was difficult to enter or leave the city. This was a 100-year "flow event," in the terms of hydrologists, and it occurred at a time of year when rain is not expected in the Sonoran Desert. So much for orderly patterns.

In the desert, rain falls on land that does not always willingly receive it. Deserts are characterized by their rocky, sandy, and often alkaline soils, with minimal plant cover. Once that soil is saturated, water runs off in prodigious quantities, collecting in streambeds normally unaccustomed to hosting much water within their banks.

Heavy runoff and uncertainty are two hallmarks of desert precipitation. The third, and perhaps most important, is evaporation. As much as seven or eight *feet* of water could potentially evaporate for every inch that falls. There just doesn't seem to be much chance for life in the desert.

The dry lands of the western United States extend from southeast California, Arizona, New Mexico, Texas, and north into Utah, small parts of Colorado, Nevada, and southern Oregon. To newcomers this is the land where lizards and snakes and other crawling, stinging animals live.

Four separate deserts have been identified—the Sonoran, Mohave, Chihuahuan, and Great Basin. All four are a function of a global climatic phenomenon. Within the latitudes where they are located, between the Tropic of Capricorn and Tropic of Cancer, is a mass of warm, descending air that holds water rather than giving it up in the form of precipitation.

Another key factor is their location in relation to mountains. Deserts valleys are bowls rimmed with young, rugged mountains. Local deserts form in the "rain shadow" of these mountains. In a larger view, all four exist because the Sierra Nevada block the passage of Pacific Ocean storms. As air hits this mountain barrier, it rises, cools and condenses. Rain and snow fall on the western side of the Sierra, and moisture rarely reaches the other side. This dry, neglected side is what, over time, has become desert.

Though they may have common origins, each of the four deserts is different. The Sonoran Desert, in southern Arizona, Baja California, and Sonora, Mexico, is the lushest of the four, receiving rainfall in two seasons—split nearly equally between winter and summer. The giant saguaro cactus, called the Great Green Spirit by writer Mary Austin, symbolizes this desert to many people.

The Mohave Desert's trademark is the bizarre Joshua tree, that gangly member of the yucca family frequently seen in magazine photos silhouetted against a flame-red sunset. The Mormons named it, because it reminded them of a biblical patriarch beckoning them across the sere desert. The Mohave, in northeast Arizona and southeast California, is the smallest and hottest of the four deserts. It also boasts the lowest elevation—282 feet below sea level in Death Valley.

The United States can barely lay claim to the Chihuahuan Desert, two-thirds of which is in Mexico. High plateaus with cool winters and hot summers best characterize its topography and climate. Almost three-fourths of its rain falls in the summer. The small portion of the Chihuahuan Desert in this country is best seen in Big Bend National Park on the Rio Grande in Texas.

The Great Basin is the coldest and highest, mostly at 4,000 feet or above in elevation and above. Snow falls on it in winter, when most precipitation visits. Streams disappear into dry sinks and salty playas with no outlets to the sea, hence its name, Great Basin. This is sagebrush country, made famous by Zane Grey, some of the biggest, emptiest land around.

The pinyon-juniper community of the Great Basin and the plateaus, though not true desert, deserves mention if only for its sheer extent in the West. These woodlands of "pygmy" trees provide the transition between desert scrub and mountain forest, and are, by any definition, dry lands.

Author Joseph Wood Krutch wrote often and well about the desert. An easterner who came to the desert late in life, he watched and listened carefully and shared what he had discovered about its mystique: "the desert is conservative, not radical. . . . The heroism which it encourages is the heroism of endurance, not that of conquest." More than any other place, the desert shows that water is the great equalizer.

Larry Ulrich

EVENING PRIMROSE & SAND VERBENA

Oenothera spp. *& Abronia* spp.

A tuft of evening primroses,/O'er which the mind may hover till it dozes;/O'er which it well might take a pleasant sleep;/But that 't is ever startled by the leap/Of buds into ripe flowers.

The sudden opening of evening primroses is said to produce a popping sound. It awakened the poet Keats to the remarkable behavior of these nocturnal flowers that decorate dry desert talus slopes and sandy places.

Most in this group unfurl their heart-shaped white or yellow petals in late day, blooming perhaps for one more day, and then fading. Their light color and pleasant fragrance attract night-flying insects, especially moths. Nectar, often at the base of a floral tube, is available only to moths with their long proboscises.

After winter rains have watered the desert, sand verbena flowers sprawl among the evening primrose in masses of pink. Sand verbena's unforgettable sweet fragrance will have you coming back time after time to renew the memory. The round flower heads consist of many small individual flowers, tubular with spreading ruffled skirts. Their fleshy leaves and sticky stems are clothed with soft hairs to inhibit evaporation of water.

4 2

PRINCE'S PLUME

Stanleya pinnata

*T*he tall leafy stems of prince's plume wave their wands of yellow flowers in many different places all over the West. They are especially fond of deserts and plains, and are frequent inhabitants of sagebrush and pinyon-juniper areas.

These showy plants grow on spurned ground. They actually prefer alkali- and gypsum-rich soils, often shaly or silty and loaded with a poisonous mineral, selenium. Prince's plume incorporates selenium and concentrates it as a substitute for sulphur.

The cooked young leaves, which have been used as a potherb, give away its family ties. They taste like cabbage, which along with all its relatives, belongs to the large mustard family. Prince's plume and cabbage may not immediately seem related, but their small, four-petaled flowers, arranged at right angles to one another, reveal their relationship.

4 4

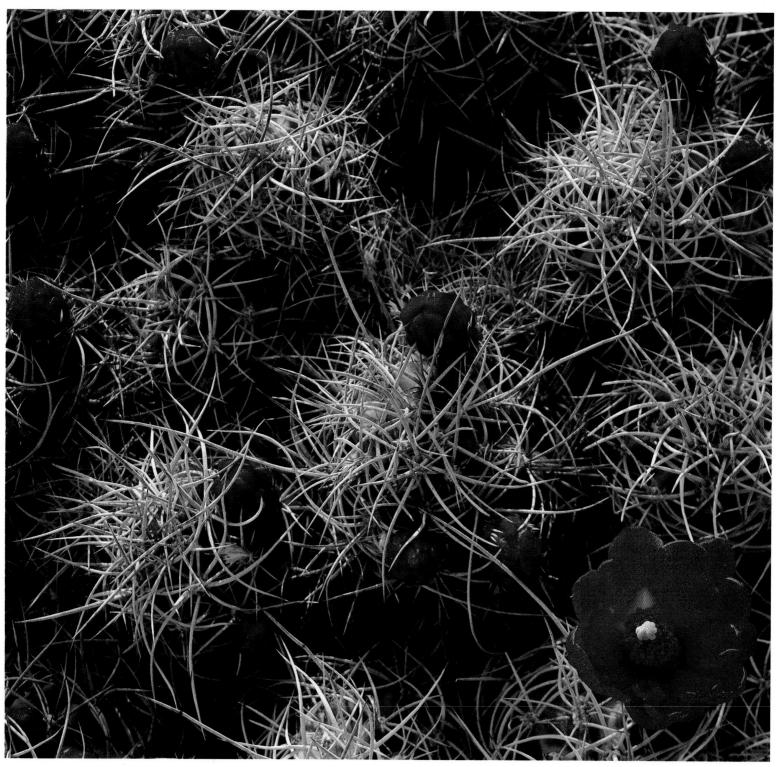

M O H A V E   M O U N D   C A C T U S

Echinocereus mohavensis

From the Mohave Desert comes this interesting cactus graced with flowers the color of a fine claret. More than five hundred stems, entangled with straw-colored spines, can huddle into a mound or clump. The tortuous spines shade the plant and protect it from animals that might want to have it for dinner.

The flowers are slender and small, producing fruits that are edible. *Echinocereus* cacti are also called strawberry cactus for the red fruits. Another oft-used name for them is hedgehog cactus.

Like most cacti, this is a perennial. It grows on dry rocky slopes and canyons in the mountains of the hottest desert in the United States, the Mohave, where surveyors charting a route for the Pacific Railway discovered it more than a century ago. The Mohave mound cactus appears on the Arizona and California sides of the lower Colorado River, and into Nevada and Utah.

Scientists have written at length about the classification of this plant. To simplify its long, complex history, suffice to say that some consider *mohavensis* one of several varieties within a species called *triglochidiatus*. The problem arises from the fact that in nature cacti tend to interbreed and evolve quickly.

4 6

Pat O'Hara

PAINTBRUSH

Castilleja spp.

In the slickrock canyon country of the Southwest, the paintbrush is one of the earliest plants to bloom, splashing bright red from crevices of rock. This plant deceives us, though. What we see is not really the flower, but colorful bracts and a calyx. The narrow small flower is hidden among the velvety outer parts.

Paintbrush earns some of its living from other plants. The roots may parasitize those of a nearby plant, sagebrush for example, and because of this fondness for a host, paintbrush are not easily transplanted.

Though red or vermilion are common colors, some paintbrushes are a sulphur yellow. The Navajo, in whose land the plant is abundant, have a word for it that means "hummingbird root." They have used fresh flowers or the entire plant to obtain a tan or greenish-yellow dye.

Most paintbrushes are perennials, and they make up a large genus of species sometimes hard to identify without a microscope and botanical key. The genus name derives from an eighteenth-century Spanish botanist, Domingo Castillejo.

One species of paintbrush is the state flower of Wyoming. They all belong to the snapdragon family, which includes penstemons and monkeyflowers.

Kathleen Norris Cook

BEAVERTAIL CACTUS

Opuntia basilaris

Metallic pink blossoms adorn the fleshy pads of the beavertail. The pads (actually stems) are what give it its name. They are flat gray-green pancakes that lack spines, a positive identifier of this species.

Beware of this seemingly cuddly cactus. Though lacking large spines, it bears hundreds of minute barbed bristles called glochids. In the understated words of one botanist, they are "troublesome." Should you happen to touch one of these plants, it can take hours to remove the glochids from a hand or leg. Glochids grow from areoles, small structures on the pads that look like dimples. Areoles are characteristic features of all cacti, and are the points from which the flower and spines grow.

The single magenta blossoms of beavertail are large, up to three inches wide, with many petals, and sepals that look much like petals. From March to June they can nearly cover the plant, providing startling color against light-colored desert soils.

Indians used all parts of this cactus for food, including the grayish-brown fruits, the flowers, and the pads.

The *Opuntia* genus, the so-called prickly pear group, is the largest of the cactus family. Pliny used the genus name, perhaps taken from the Greek city Opus.

DATURA

Datura spp.

A nts look like horses and butterflies like airplanes." This is how a Pima Indian described the effects of the datura root on those who chewed even a small piece of it.

The vision-inducing powers of datura have long been known to Indians in the Southwest and Mexico. Sacred datura or jimson weed are other common names for this large, coarse plant with the trumpet-shaped flowers. A brew called toloache (an Aztec word) is made from the crushed root or seeds, a drink that was a key ingredient in initiation rites for boys and girls entering adulthood. To the Navajo it is the plant "that looks like a banana," one they believe makes people crazy.

The active hallucinatory substances are atropine, scopolomine, and hyoscyamine. All parts of the plant are narcotic or poisonous, both to people and to livestock. Datura is of the potato family, which includes a number of well-known plants—chilies, tomatoes, potatoes, eggplants, and tobacco.

From a closed spiral, datura buds unfold in the evening, and the flowers stay open through the night. The flowers are white, sometimes tinged with lavender, yielding fruits with large prickly, globe-shaped seedpods, hence its other familiar name, thornapple. It is a summer-bloomer, and the sweet fragrance and white "glow" of the flowers attracts nocturnal moths. The lush foliage, however, has been likened to the smell of a wet dog.

SEGO OR MARIPOSA LILY

Calochortus spp.

Beautiful grass," its name means in Greek. This member of the lily family presents exquisitely marked flowers atop slender grasslike leaves. The sego lily is usually white, sometimes coloring to lavender or pink. In California, which is rich in species of *Calochortus*, an intense orange mariposa lily grows. Nestled at the base of each of the three broad petals are dark spots or glands, sometimes adorned with hair. These markings may have led the Spanish to use their word for butterfly, mariposa.

Flowers of the desert, they show a preference for sandy, dry soil, and are found on plains, among sagebrush, and in pinyon-juniper and other open pine forests of arid regions.

The sego lily (*C. nuttalli*) is the state flower of Utah. It is common outside cities, threatened only "by enthusiastic wildflower collectors or an occasionally hungry cow," according to the authors of *Intermountain Flora*.

Among the people of the region, the flower has a long history. Southwest Indians ate the small bulb of the sego lily, and they taught Mormon settlers of its edibility. The Indians believed the sego lily was a gift from the Great Spirit in answer to their prayers that their hot dry land be made prosperous. They called it the "life plant" of the hills. The bulb is said to be about the size of a walnut and to have the taste of a potato.

54

PRICKLY POPPY

Argemone spp.

The papery thin flower petals are the only thing about the prickly poppy that could be called delicate. This is a tough, drought-resistant plant that prefers places "where the world goes by." You will see them frequently in summer along roads, in old fields, and in overgrazed pastures.

Spiny-edged leaves, stems, and seedpods keep away most anything that might wish to tamper with it. All parts of *Argemone* are poisonous, and the seeds are said to be more narcotic than even the opium poppy, to which it is related. Seeds and leaves contain toxic alkaloids.

The bitter yellow or orange sap that prickly poppies exude reportedly cured cataracts. The Greek word *argema* means "cataract of the eye." Other common names include *chicalote*, indicative of the plant's Mexican heritage, and thistle poppy, for its spiny defenses. The Mexican prickly poppy has bright yellow petals. California's matilija poppy, with showy large white flowers, is highly similar, and some consider it more spectacular.

The poppy family includes plants native to Europe, North Africa, Asia, and the western United States. The most famous member is the opium poppy, either a drug or a poison, depending on dose.

G I L I A

Ipomopsis spp.

Scarlet gilia, desert trumpet, fire pink, polecat plant, and skunk flower are all colloquial names for this outstanding plant. From the slender tube at the base of the flower, the five petals flare out like fireworks, giving it yet another appropriate name, skyrocket. Often intensely red, the flowers can also be pink or mottled with white specks.

On some species the flowers stand out from the top of loosely branched, tall stems. They sometimes completely cover dry slopes, from the canyon lands, to sagebrush, to open forest. Skyrocket ranges far and wide in the western states, from eastern Oregon to southern California and east to Texas, blooming in early summer after the first rains. A biennial or perennial, it grows readily from seed.

Hummingbirds and moths don't seem to mind the skunky smell of the foliage. Pronghorn, deer, and other grazing animals like to eat it.

"Gilia" honors eighteenth-century Spanish botanist Felipe Gil. Those who adhere to the Spanish pronounce the "g" softly—"hilia."

S omeone once said that "Landscape is geology with plants on it." This might be revised somewhat to say that "Mountains are geology with plants on them."

At first sight, from a distance, the great mountain ranges of the western United States appear to be masses of bare rock. These are the mountains whose glaciated peaks extend for hundreds of miles north-south across the country. They are of different origins and ages—the Sierra Nevada's smooth-arching granite domes, the Cascades' chocolate volcanic rock, and the Rocky Mountains' twisted and complex sedimentary faces. Glaciers long ago etched and carved their upper reaches into lakes and valleys and sharp ridges. The highest peaks, many of which soar to 14,000 feet above sea level, are always in close range of winter.

What counts in the mountains is elevation. Their height makes them magnets for moisture-laden air masses, usually from the Pacific Ocean. As warm air rises over them, it cools and condenses. So mountains regularly receive rain and snow.

In the mountains we say that the air is thin—because the higher we go the harder it becomes to draw a breath. It is the air, said Mark Twain, that the angels breathe. Indeed, oxygen is less plentiful at high altitudes, causing the unacclimated to give their bodies time to adjust. We know too that in the high mountains summers are short. The higher we go, the cooler it is. As a rule of thumb, for every thousand feet gained in altitude, temperature drops three degrees Fahrenheit. This rule is especially significant to plants that inhabit mountains.

Continued on page 62

Daisies and aspen forest

(opposite page) by Jeff Gnass,

camas lily (far right)

by Tom and Pat Leeson

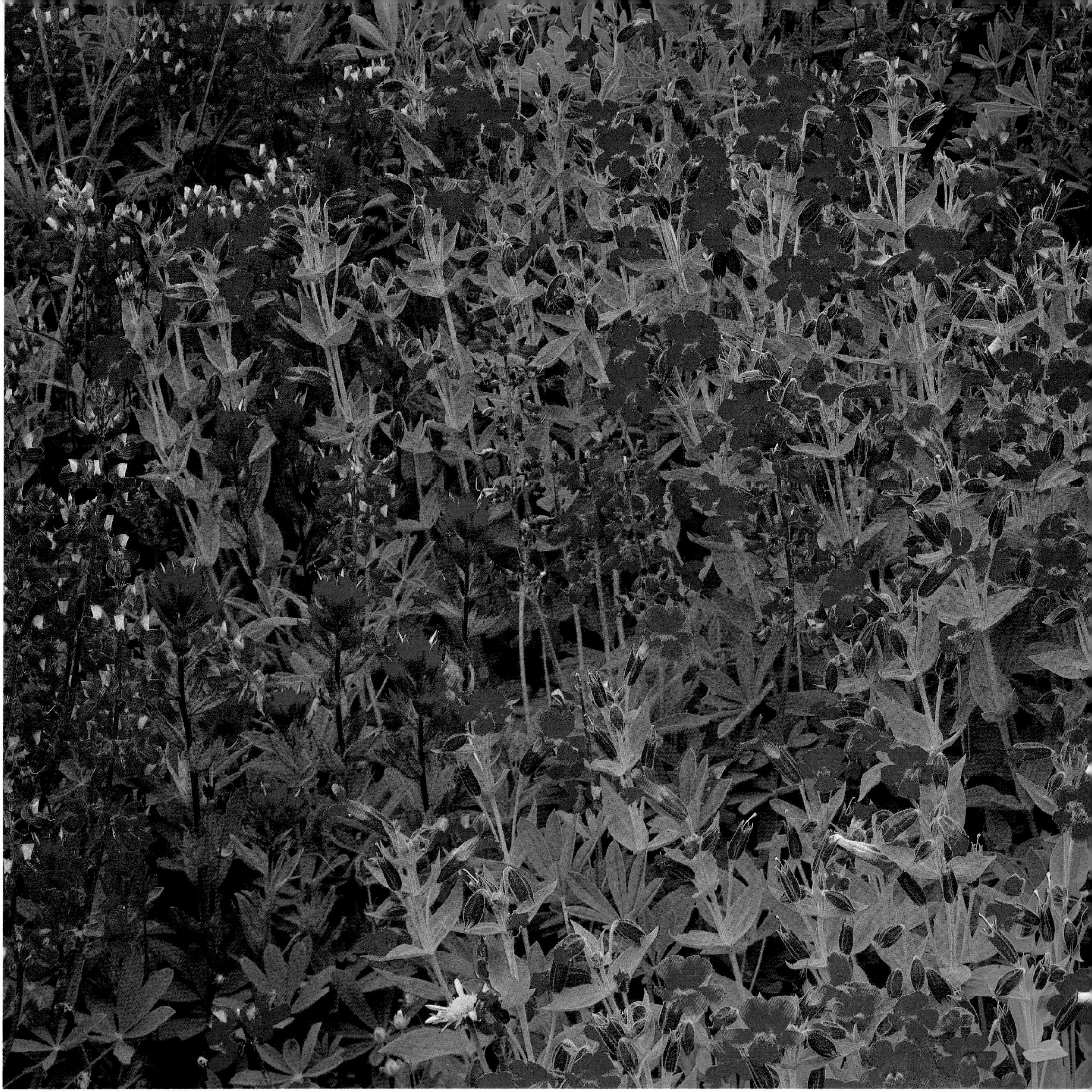

Pat O'Hara

M O N K E Y F L O W E R

Mimulus spp.

*E*ven the most calloused observer of nature cannot help but smile back at the monkeyflower's grinning face. *Mimulus*, the "little mimic," is the clown of the mountains. The upper and lower lips of the flower tell of its family affiliation. It belongs to the snapdragon or figwort family, which also includes foxglove, toadflax, paintbrush and penstemons. Monkeyflowers are all-Americans, with most species found from the Rocky Mountains west.

The rich pink, red, and rose colors of *Mimulus lewisii* shine beside cold streams and other wet places in the mountains. The bright flowers contrast with their lush green leaves. Yellow markings on the flower's throat, sometimes dotted with freckles, create the "grin" that makes monkeyflowers irresistible. Captain Meriwether Lewis, William Clark's sidekick, is honored in its name.

In summer after the trout have spawned, monkeyflowers bloom amid alpine gardens of red paintbrush and blue lupines. By the time their petals have dropped into the streams, the trout are moving to deeper downstream waters for the winter.

Other monkeyflowers, found also on the coast and in deserts, are yellow and orange or scarlet.

In the last century a scientist named C. Hart Merriam applied these everyday facts about mountains and worked out a simple scheme that divided the West into life zones. Merriam's zones were based primarily on elevation, and changes in plantlife going up a mountainside. To experience the zones, one could travel from Sonora, Mexico, to the Arctic. But Merriam discovered that equivalent changes could be seen in a journey of only sixty miles, from the bottom of the Grand Canyon to the top of the San Francisco Peaks outside Flagstaff, Arizona.

Six of North America's seven major zones occur within that part of Arizona—lower Sonoran desert at the bottom of the Grand Canyon, upper Sonoran at the canyon rim, the Transition forest of ponderosa pine on the plateau leading to Flagstaff. Continuing on to the San Francisco Peaks, one would encounter three additional plant communities—the Canadian (spruce-fir forest), Hudsonian (subalpine), and finally alpine tundra above treeline.

Merriam's concept still works, especially in the mountains of the West. Other researchers have since refined his idea, and complicating factors have been introduced. The hypothetical neat boundary lines of each life zone are in reality blurred somewhat by variables such as moisture, soil, slope angle, exposure to sun and wind, and others. Nevertheless, similarities are evident among plants of the Rocky Mountains, Sierras, Cascades, and the Southwest's so-called "mountain islands" and high plateaus. Though individual species vary from mountain range to mountain range, even with a passing knowledge of life zones the patterns of plant distribution and their normal environments begin to fall into place.

Alpine tundra makes a good example. Tundra is found on high-mountain summits, above treeline. The word itself evokes images of its origins: Russian steppe and the barren hills of Finland. Life here is lived on the edge, and anything that survives does so out of eons of adaptation.

Alpine plants everywhere face the same challenges. They must keep their pollen dry, find perhaps an insect to act as a pollinator, weather constant cold and wind, locate even a dab of soil to sink roots into, and survive heaving frost and intense sun. No wonder that there are only 300 species of tundra plants known in Colorado, and about half that number in tundra in other parts of the country.

How do they do it, these hardiest yet most fragile of mountain beings? One major and noticeable way is by becoming dwarfs. They hug the ground as petite cushions and rosettes no larger than a penny, protecting themselves against winds that can blow 120 miles an hour. Stems are almost out of the question, and leaves are small, often smooth and waxy. Hairs of all descriptions—bristly, silky, sticky, wavy, and pubescent—trap heat and warm the plant. In this way, they are like desert plants in their strategies for regulating temperature and saving water. The difference is that desert plants try to keep cool, whereas tundra plants want to stay warm.

Deep roots enable alpine plants to hold on to rocks, and snow, the major source of water, is their security blanket, burying them so that they can survive the winter, which starts early and stays late.

Though certainly counted among some of the most beautiful flowers in the world, these alpine lovelies must be frugal. Annuals are almost absent. They cannot afford to bloom and go to seed in the short capricious season that the tundra calls summer. Instead, almost all are perennials, and some will wait at least a decade to bloom. They have no soft, fleshy parts and the flat-faced flowers are always small. They grow in masses, to show off for the flies and bees that will spread their pollen. They are truly marvels, these tough flowers with the whimsical names—candytuft and columbine, avens and forget-me-not, Easter daisy and chiming bell.

Alpine tundra is by definition treeless. Treeline, timberline, or treelimit—all the same thing—is the highest elevation at which trees grow. In the Northern Hemisphere, it closely follows the line where mean summer temperatures average 50 degrees Fahrenheit. In the southern Rockies treeline elevation is around 11,500 to 12,000 feet; farther north in the Montana Rockies, the limits are lower, around 7,500 feet.

Basically, trees cannot grow above treeline because it is too cold. According to Ann Zwinger and Beatrice Willard in their book *Land Above the Trees*, only enough heat is available to meet the trees' respiratory requirements, renew their needles, and produce a small band of wood. They usually do not set seed or have cones. The distinctive gnarled shape of trees here is called "krummholz," the German word for elfin timber or crooked wood. At treeline trees more closely resemble twisted, prostrate shrubs. Their tops are flat or flagged, and their windward side is almost always devoid of branches.

Below treeline begin the extensive swaths of conifer forests—the pines and spruces and firs—for which the western mountains are perhaps best known. Their decaying needles and branches and cones add to the soil layers in the forest. In some cases, at least with lodgepole pines, this presents a great handicap to flowers, because tannins and resins in the needles can hinder the growth of plants at the base of these trees.

These coniferous forests embrace three of Merriam's life zones: Hudsonian, Canadian, and Transition. The Hudsonian or subalpine habitat of the high Sierra is a rocky environment, home to whitebark pine. Here red heather, Sierra stonecrop, and western roseroot have adapted to the warm summer days and always cool nights. In the Rockies the subalpine forest is made up of Engelmann spruce, limber pine, and subalpine fir.

The Canadian zone, too, is cool, with heavy snows common from November to May in the Sierras. Red snowplant lines the edges of melting snowbanks in spring, followed by tiger lilies along streamsides in August and September. Red fir, lodgepole pine, and mountain hemlock are characteristic evergreens in the Canadian-zone forests. Jeffrey pine, Douglas fir, sugar pine, and incense cedar, among others, take over in the lower parts of this zone in the Sierras and Cascades.

In the open, drier parts of the mountains and at lower elevations—the Transition zone—ponderosa pine becomes more common. John Muir, archdruid of the mountains, ranked ponderosa pine second in the lineup of great forest trees. The sweet vanilla scent permeating a ponderosa forest on a warm summer day is intoxicating. On such a day, should you happen to see a gorgeous shooting star, its striking pink flower reaching heavenward, you will wish to be nowhere else on earth.

Wildflowers sometimes have trouble getting the sunlight they need in the shaded forest. A few, like pinedrops and snowplant, have no chlorophyll, thus eliminating the need to have sun to photosynthesize. With a few exceptions, such as the trillium of the rainforest, many flowers find meadows and clearings more suited to their needs.

Mr. Muir extolled the virtues of the mountain meadow, "one of Nature's most sacred chambers." These wild lawns, he wrote, are "so brightly enameled with flowers and butterflies that it may well be called a garden-meadow or meadow-garden." Gentians in three different shades of blue, daisies, yellow ivesias, penstemons, and clover crowd out the grasses in places. Mountain meadows are former glacial lakes that slowly dried up and filled in with grasses and mosses and herbs. Within their unspoiled expanses, brooks and bogs provide homes for water-loving flowers and shrubs.

For many reasons mountains, probably more than any other place, offer the greatest possibilities for wildflowers. Differences in elevation, abundant water, clear air, light, and temperature together create a richness irresistible to flowers and those who love them. 🌱

C O L U M B I N E

Aquilegia spp.

F ringing the stream, peering over the bank, as if to see its own loveliness reflected there, or hiding in the greenest recesses of the woodland," the columbine is a blossom that upon beholding it brightens the eye and quickens the pulse. Mary Elizabeth Parsons at the turn of the century was describing the red and yellow species that grows abundantly in California's mountain meadows.

An equally lilting description could apply to another familiar columbine, *Aquilegia coerulea*, the breathtaking blue and white species well known to Rocky Mountain travelers. By a referendum of the state's school children it was crowned the Colorado flower. During summer, troupes of columbines kick up their heels and dance under fluttering green tents of aspen groves. At one time a movement was afoot to designate the columbine the national flower, though it never came to pass.

Chaucer was fond of columbines and used them as symbols in his poetry. One of its old names is "lion's herb," because it was curiously believed to be a favorite plant of lions. In medieval times columbines were a suggested remedy against plague. *Banke's Herbal* of 1525 says "columbina's virtue is good for him that hath the quinsy. This herb must be gathered in August." Seeds of at least one species could be crushed and brewed into a tea, good for headache and fever. A tea of the steeped roots and leaves could relieve stomach troubles.

Pat O'Hara, (*opposite page*) Tom and Pat Leeson

BALSAMROOT
PRAIRIE STAR & LADY'S SLIPPER

Balsamorhiza spp., *Lithophragma* spp. & *Cypripedium* spp.

*L*ike the sun among the stars, the large flowers of balsamroot grow in a grassy field amid prairie stars (*facing page*). These flowers share the same blooming time, from April to August. Both prefer dry ground among sagebrush and ponderosa pine forests, on mountain ridges and high plateaus. Oregon Indians called balsamroot *posh* or *kayoum*, and Utah pioneers knew it as Mormon biscuit. The root is edible when its pungent bark is removed. Prairie star is a member of the saxifrage family, the "rock breakers." The five dainty white to pale pink petals, growing from nearly leafless slender stems, seem suspended from the sky by an invisible string.

The lady's slipper (*this page*) is a showy orchid that ranges in color from yellow, to greenish with white lips, brownish, and purplish. When he came upon it in his walks, John Burroughs said, "I seem to be intruding upon some very private and exclusive company." Today they are even rarer, due to thoughtless collectors.

Orchids are the flowers of love, and earliest legends repeatedly attributed aphrodisiac qualities to them. Orchis was a passionate satyr who created an uproar at a feast by bothering one of the priestesses. For his indiscretions he was dismembered by the angry celebrants. Despite his father's prayers, the gods let him die, though mercifully they changed him into a flower. Hence the name of the orchid family and one of its genera.

Pat O'Hara

B E L L F L O W E R

Campanula rotundifolia

We have a choice of names for this flower—bellflower, bluebell, or harebell, among others. Its blue, to lavender, to white flowers, hanging like wedding bells from the tops of the stems, are responsible for the "bell" in its appellations. *Campanula* in Latin means "little bell," which is also the origin of the name of its widespread family, Campanulaceae.

The "hare" of harebell goes back to old England and Scotland and to witches. Many plants in those days had the name "hare" in them. If a hare crossed your path it meant bad luck, because witches could turn themselves into hares. And harebells were believed to be witches' thimbles.

Bellflowers are especially adaptable to an assortment of habitats, from foothills to alpine areas. *Gray's Manual of Botany* notes that they readily respond to "slight changes in aridity, moisture, nutriment, and exposure." Bellflowers can be found in meadows and on rocky slopes in nearly all the high mountains.

During his travels in Alaska, John Muir spied them and wrote these exulting words: ". . . though frail and delicate-looking, none of its companions is more enduring or rings out the praise of beauty-loving Nature in tones more appreciable to mortals."

The round leaves at their base usually wither before the bluebells bloom. Look for these flowers from June to September.

SHOOTING STAR

Dodecatheon spp.

From one biased viewpoint, shooting stars are among the most beautiful flowers on earth. Others must have partly agreed, for one species bears the name *pulchellum*, which in Latin means "pretty" or "beautiful." Letting his imagination run wild, Linnaeus saw in their blooms a convention of gods seated around Olympus; hence the genus name *Dodecatheon*, from the Greek *dodeka*, twelve, and *theoi*, gods.

The flowers are reddish purple, pink, magenta, lavender, and occasionally white. The dark center cone, often ringed with yellow, contains the anther-bearing stamens.

Shooting stars hang upside down on the tip of slender stems, like umbrellas turned inside out by the wind. This growth habit presents challenges to bees, usually bumblebees, that come to dine on pollen and nectar. The flower offers no landing platform, and consequently a bee must cling to the cone at the base of the flower. While in this contortion, the bee, flapping its wings, shakes pollen free from the cone. The pollen grains fall onto its abdomen and stick there, to be transported during the bee's travels to another shooting star.

Several species of shooting stars grace our mountains, most often in meadows, along streams, and on wet ground. They bloom from June to August. In the fall the seedpods look like brown brooms, observed naturalist Ann Zwinger, and retain the structure of the flower blossoms that preceded them.

Larry Ulrich

SNEEZEWEED

Helenium spp.

Cold-sufferers rejoice! If you sniff a handful of dried, pulverized sneezeweed, you will sneeze your way out of a stuffy head cold. At least that is one alleged benefit of this plant and tells us how it got its name. Those allergic to the pollen may not find it so beneficent.

Sneezeweeds, part of that giant family known as composites, have toothed, orange-yellow ray flowers that look like petals, surrounding a spherical disk of minute flowers. The large flower heads top stout, tall stems that sometimes reach four feet in height.

These flowers prefer wet or damp places—mountain meadows in the Sierras and the west slope of the Rockies, or around swamps and on bluffs of the northern California and southern Oregon coasts.

Ranchers have found that heavily grazed areas are a favorite of sneezeweeds as well, causing serious problems among their sheep. A poisonous glycoside in the plant accumulates in the animals and causes "spewing sickness."

This late summer and fall flower owes its genus name to Helen of Troy, according to the "Prince of Botany," Carolus Linnaeus.

Kathleen Norris Cook, *(opposite page)* Pat O'Hara

LARKSPUR & GLACIER LILY

Delphinium spp. *& Erythronium* spp.

The heel, toe, spur, and claw of the lark have all been used as common names for this widespread genus (*facing page*). The hollow tube extending back from the uppermost of the flower's five sepals is the spur. In most species the flowers range from blue to purple, though a lovely white larkspur grows in the Plains, and a scarlet one is known in California woods.

All parts of this beautiful plant are poisonous. It contains a number of alkaloids, delphinine being among the worst. When cattle eat the fresh green plants in the spring, they suffer weakness, nausea, and death. Larkspur has been used as an insecticide, and soldiers at one time applied it externally to kill body lice.

The graceful glacier lily (*this page*) blooms in high mountain forests in the summer, tagging after the melting snowfields and sometimes covering entire meadows with their yellow or white blossoms.

The glacier lily first appears as a shy, drooping bud, but as it opens, the flower stretches for the sky. The six petal-like segments curve back, which may explain a rather misleading common name, dogtooth violet. Mottling on the oblong leaves— or perhaps because blossoms come forth about the time that deer begin to fawn— has earned it a fairer name, fawn lily.

Indians boiled and ate the bulbs of this and other lilies. The cooked seedpods are said to resemble green beans in flavor. Grizzly and black bears also gather and eat the bulbs.

Larry Ulrich

PARRY'S PRIMROSE

Primula parryi

Parry's primrose "is one of the best reasons for climbing mountains," says botanist Harold William Rickett. He may be right. This plant, known for its height, grows along brooks in the high mountains of the West, from June to August. The striking magenta-pink blooms and yellow "eye" at the center are distinctive and noticeable.

Charles Christopher Parry encountered this flower in the Rocky Mountains in the 1860s, during one of his summer expeditions. English-born and trained as a physician, Parry spent most of his adult life in America. He named Gray's Peak in the Rockies for one of his contemporaries, the great botanist Asa Gray. Gray in turn described this primrose and named it after his colleague.

Parry's primrose is endemic to our western mountains, which means that it is found nowhere else in the world. An alpine species, the fairy primrose, grows here, and a small species is found in the Sierra Nevada. These flowers belong to the "true" primrose family, as distinguished from the evening primroses, which are in a different family.

Many people comment on the odor of this beautiful flower—it smells like carrion, possibly a lure to certain insects, especially flies, that are attracted to such scents.

C A L Y P S O

Calypso bulbosa

Calypso was a sea nymph, a goddess, and queen of the island of Ogygia. To readers of Homer's *Odyssey*, she is remembered as the one who waylaid Odysseus for seven years.

Like the goddess for whom it is named, the calypso orchid finds secluded places to its liking. Some searching among duff and moss in woods is required to find the solitary flowers, each one carried delicately at the top of a stem with a single leaf springing from the base. The flower is mostly pink, with reddish-purple spots and stripes on the lower lip, and a beard of yellow hairs.

One of the three petals forms a lip, often looking like an inflated sack. Its function is to secrete nectar to attract insects. The style, stigma, and stamens form what is called a column in the center of the flower. This column, and the lip, are unique to orchids. As the specialized orchids evolved, the ovary made a half turn, so what was originally the bottom of the flower is now the top.

Botanist Leslie L. Haskin noted that in the Northwest "These flowers delight in the full shade of fir woods where they stand embedded, not in soil, but in deep mosses. Often they will be found growing in close ranks upon the mossy trunks of fallen trees." He mentions another local name for calypso, the deer-head orchid.

Larry Ulrich

G E N T I A N

Gentiana spp.

C an a flower so deeply blue be anything but the reflection of a western sky in autumn? Gentians are "Heaven's own blue," proclaimed editor and nature poet William Cullen Bryant.

A variety of gentians adorns meadows and stream edges in the mountains in late summer and fall. Their funnel-form flowers, fringed or pleated, stand on the stems like purple chalices.

The fringed gentian, an annual, is a rare beauty. In 1926 Yellowstone National Park selected it as the park flower. Its sensitivity to light and temperature is keen, and without the sun, the flower goes into hiding. Another species, the bottle gentian, is noted for never opening its petals.

Gentius, King of Illyria, lived from 180 to 167 B.C. He is said to have been the first to discover the flower's medicinal values, though knowledge of gentians perhaps dates back another thousand years, recorded on papyrus in a tomb at Thebes. Therapeutic virtues attributed to the gentian were myriad—"It is one of the best strengtheners of the human system," declared one herbalist. A tonic was made of the root, commonly of a yellow species. One of its old English names was "bitterwort," attesting to the bitterness of the concoction. Fermented, it made brandy, wine, or liqueur.

Joe Arnold

L O U S E W O R T

Pedicularis spp.

Wort" is simply from the Old English word for plant or root. The "louse" appended to it relates to an antique belief associated with this plant. Farmers once thought that if their cattle or sheep ate lousewort, they would contract lice—a slanderous view of these interesting flowers, to be sure.

Among the five hundred or so species of *Pedicularis* in the world, primarily in the north temperate zone, fascinating flower architectures have developed. Many have flowers that are on spikes or packed in dense rows on a stalk. Each flower is two-lipped, with the upper one commonly folded lengthwise or forming a beak. One species of our western mountains, elephant's head, is so named because the upper lip extends out in an exaggeration that looks remarkably like the trunk of a pachyderm.

In the mountains louseworts are frequently found in wet areas from middle-elevation coniferous forests to alpine tundra. Yellow is a common color, but they also range from cream and white to pink and purple. The leaves are often fernlike.

All of their fancy structures are in some way related to pollination. Devices like the flower's upper beak protect the pistil and the anther-bearing stamens. The lower lip, a landing pad for insects, places them in a position for pollen to be shaken onto them. However, in trying to locate nectar in the complicated flowers, some frustrated insects resort to biting off the end of the corolla to get at the nectar.

*T*o be prairie, really good prairie, it must embrace the horizons." John Madson, author and prairie lover, defined his home this way. The sky unimpeded by trees, and acres upon acres of flowing grass, are the essence of the prairie. If we think about it, all the excesses and elements of the prairie come from the sky. Sun, wind, lightning, blizzards, grasshoppers. Always the sky.

The extreme openness of this land bothers some people. Many try to avoid the prairie, finding it monotonous and bland. They drive across it in the night, hurrying for the mountains and hoping to bypass the boredom the flat land brings on. They may have basis for their opinions. There is a portion of west Texas called the Staked Plains, a landscape so featureless that early explorers and settlers pounded stakes in the ground to mark their way.

In all fairness, what we see today is not really the prairie. Mere scraps are left. Only the Indians and early explorers had the good fortune to see the original version with all its shadings and subtleties. To them it was the edge of the world.

Hard as it may be for us to grasp today, the *true* prairie was America's midsection—Illinois, Iowa, parts of Missouri, Minnesota, the eastern Dakotas and Nebraska and Kansas—now the nation's breadbasket where corn and soft winter wheat thrive. This was once tallgrass prairie, where big bluestem proverbially grew as high as a man. The prairie landscape lacked any connection with the thick green forests of the Appalachians and the Mississippi River bottomlands that had been home to the pioneers.

Gaillardia and buttercups

(opposite page) by David Muench,

coneflower (far right)

by Charles E. Schmidt

The French, the first to write of it, liked this country that extended unendingly, as far as the eye could see. They were the first to call it "prairie," their word for a grassy orchard or park.

Some Americans, however, among them Zebulon Pike and Lewis and Clark, sent home less than enthusiastic reports of the Louisiana Purchase, the country's newly acquired real estate beyond the Mississippi. But others found it striking, gay, and exhilarating. "The flowers, so fragile, so delicate, and so ornamented seem to have been tastefully disposed to adorn the scene," cooed one poetic soul.

Easterners chose to believe the glowing accounts, and headed west en masse in the mid-1800s. They broke the tallgrass prairie with their plows, made roofs for their houses from the thick sod, and then they went farther, into yet a different kind of prairie, the mixed grass and shortgrass. It is to this land, the Great Plains, that we turn our attention.

The Great Plains—the West—begin at the one hundredth meridian, a line that runs from north to south through the United States. It bisects the Dakotas, Nebraska, and Kansas, follows the eastern edge of the Oklahoma-Texas Panhandle, and hits the border around Brownsville.

The hundredth meridian marks a momentous meteorological change. West of it, rainfall is less than twenty inches a year. To farmers it means that corn will no longer grow with the blessing of rain, but instead irrigated wheat or grazing land are the options. The traveler crossing the country here leaves the humid East and enters the West. "There is," wrote photographer David Plowden, "an ever increasing dryness to the air, a lustier tempo in the wind; the presence of a larger sky, the opportunity for a longer view."

The land rises as you proceed westward, from about 2,500 feet to a mile above sea level where the Great Plains swing up to the Rocky Mountains. Though the word "featureless" is most often used in describing the Plains, the topography does offer some variety. Canyons, buttes, badlands, benches, and alkaline valleys make a dent in the overall effect of flatness. And just to prove to nonbe-

lievers that there are mountains on the Plains, Harney Peak in the Black Hills of South Dakota soars to a majestic 7,242 feet. Still, the High Plains, a subset of the Great Plains, is acknowledged as some of the flattest terrain on earth.

The lower rainfall and higher elevation give the Great Plains an environment markedly different from the prairie to the east. The high sod-forming grasses of the tallgrass prairie like the big bluestem eventually yield to the mixed and shorter grasses, including blue grama, buffalo grass, western wheatgrass, and needlegrass. If you can't tell a blue grama from a big bluestem, observe the size of the sunflowers along the road. The farther west you go, the shorter the stems and smaller the flowers.

There's no such thing as usual weather on the Plains, it's all unusual; at least that's what the old-timers say. Undeniably, it is a place of extremes. Tornadoes, droughts, blizzards. Even from day to night, the difference in temperature is striking, primarily because of a lack of water vapor in the atmosphere. Summer highs have topped out above 100 degrees Fahrenheit, and winter lows of 40 below zero (at least on the northern plains) are "not infrequent." Storms from the Gulf of Mexico bring rain in June, while December and January are the driest months.

Drought is a phenomenon that has been part of the natural history of the Plains for longer than human memory. Though the newspapers may proclaim the latest drought the worst on record, only our short recall makes us think so. Drought has an established cycle, occurring as frequently as every five years, some say.

Prairie soils owe their richness to the masses of grass roots—sod—that fertilize the upper layers as they decompose. Because the roots decay quickly, they replenish the soil at a healthy rate. But Great Plains soils are less fertile than the rich black loam found in Iowa, and are instead pale brown in color. It has been called "chestnut" soil.

Despite all these descriptive characteristics, what really makes the prairie the prairie? The nagging question of why all grass and no trees has long been debated but not completely answered.

Various reasons have been offered: scanty rainfall, evaporation, overly fine soil or soil that lacks certain nutrients, drainage or lack thereof, age of the land, fire, or perhaps ice. The evaporation argument seems to hold most favor now. By dividing annual rainfall by rate of evaporation, values can be obtained for various regions. When plotted on a map, these ratios correspond well with where prairie is found. Put much too simply, if more water evaporates than falls, grasses are likely to prevail over trees.

Fire, though it may not make prairie, has historically and prehistorically been an integral part of maintaining the grasslands. If you were to start a prairie garden of your own, experts would advise you to burn it after the first three or four years, to clear out thatch, thin excess growth, and leave a rich ash layer for the soil. Indians burned the prairies, and called the fires "Red Buffalo." White settlers did the same, though they trenched around their fields and houses and prayed that the wind didn't come up. Before people were around, lightning, especially in late summer and fall, ignited the fires. It still does. How do the fires help preserve grasslands and prevent succession to woodlands? Grasses, which represent many fewer years of growth than trees, can squander their growth more readily. Their roots survive, and in only a year or two, grass plants and their seeds will be back. Trees face a much greater struggle over a longer time to establish themselves.

Not only do they manage to outcompete trees after a fire, prairie grasses are also experts at dealing with the sun and the wind. Their long straight leaves bend with the wind: "Tish-ah!" was how O. E. Rölvaag described their sound in his epic novel of the prairie, *Giants in the Earth*. In the slanting rays of early and late sun, grasses become silver and golden ribbons, but when the sun is high, the light falls between them and cannot burn them. Silicon oxide reinforces the outer covering of slender grass stems and keeps them tough and upright.

Grasses are flowering plants too. They are pollinated by wind, an especially desirable feature on the Plains, where wind is always plentiful. They can reproduce not only by their seeds (which are, in many cases, spread by wind) but also through their root systems. Because grass grows from the base rather than the top, it can be broken off at the tip and still live. During the extremes of winter, grasses die back to their roots and continue their work underground. Some prairie grasses are built so that during drought the leaves roll up, exposing the lower surfaces, which do not transpire water.

Though they are the original prairie survivors, grasses must compete with one another for light, water, and nutrients. Over time, each has carved its own niche. Some grow in damp swales, others on the drier hillsides. If one year is especially dry, one kind of grass will grow; in wetter years another will take a turn. Also, the roots of different species tap different layers in the soil so that not all will be clamoring for the same moisture.

Wildflowers must compete directly with the grasses as well, and they've had to outsmart them. Pasque flower or anemone, for example, blooms early in the spring and avoids the taller grasses that would soon shade it out. Later wildflowers let the summer grasses shade them from drying winds and sun. Flowers that need the sun send up a tall stem before spending precious energy on making leaves or flowers.

Other spring prairie flowers are the blue-eyed grass, buttercups, and bird's foot violets. They must hurry along, though, to make way for their leggier summer sisters—the Turk's cap lilies, butterfly weed, blazing star, purple coneflower, and prairie larkspur. By late summer, the flowers have gone all out. The great common sunflower—the prairie trademark—has exceeded fifteen feet in height in places, with a bevy of others of its genus nearby.

Autumn can be marked more surely by goldenrods and gentians than by the calendar; by the first hard frost they've joined with all the others in donning the prairie's somber winter garb, returning the land to grass and sky.

Jim Brandenburg

GAYFEATHER

Liatris spp.

No doubt on the edge of her garden a pioneer woman caught sight of the glowing purple blooms of gayfeather and was ecstatic to see their brightness, flaunting summer's final days.

Gayfeather sports rose-lavender or purple flowers densely crowded on a tall spire. This is a composite, the immense family of plants that send botanists into a tizzy over their complexities. Gayfeather, or *Liatris*, has only disk flowers, with no surrounding ray flowers. Depending on the species, one flower head may bear from four to forty disk flowers.

A perennial, gayfeather grows from a corm or bulb that was valuable winter food for Indians. The corm was also good for a sore throat and was considered an antidote to snakebite venom. This explains the origin of the name of one species of gayfeather, button snakeroot. Plains folklore tells that Indians fed the root to their horses to increase the animals' speed and endurance, an important virtue among those skilled equestrians. Dotted gayfeather is so called for the purplish glands that dot the leaves.

A lover of sandy dry soils and open places, gayfeather is especially good at resisting drought, with roots of the Plains species extending sixteen feet into the soil!

CONEFLOWER

Rudbeckia spp.

*I*n honor of his mentor Olaf Rudbeck, Swedish botanist Carolus Linnaeus named the genus *Rudbeckia*. This *Rudbeckia* is one of a multitude of members of the composite family, with daisylike blooms that are actually many flowers on one head. Composites are often considered outcasts and renegades because they are so prolific and common. Perhaps 25,000 composite species populate the world, owing much of their success to their ability to produce so many seeds.

Composites contribute their fair share to the GNP of the green world. They are important biologically and economically for they include food plants such as lettuce, artichokes and sunflowers, and ubiquitous ornamental flowers like chrysanthemums, dahlias, and marigolds.

The flower heads of *Rudbeckia* are at the top of tall, coarse stems, and they decorate open woods and fields of the Plains states from summer into fall. The yellow ray flowers point down, away from the greenish-yellow disk. There are about two dozen native species of *Rudbeckia* in North America, including the familiar favorite, black-eyed Susan.

Many prairie flowers are called coneflowers, for their center disks, and they can be difficult to tell apart. True coneflowers are now placed in another genus, and their ray flowers tend to droop more.

9 2

David Muench

TEXAS BLUEBONNET

Lupinus spp.

*I*t took a while, but Texas has solved the problem of which bluebonnet is really the official state flower. In 1901, with little debate, the legislature crowned the sandyland bluebonnet as the flower they would call their own. But this species was small and not so widespread, and most folks called another, *Lupinus texensis*, the Texas bluebonnet. To simplify the situation, in 1971 all species of *Lupinus* that occur naturally in the state became the state flower, or should we say, flowers?

The bluebonnet is a lupine, a member of what Harold William Rickett calls "one of the great families of plants," the bean or pea family. Among the some 10,000 lupine species are valuable plants like peas, peanuts, beans, clover, and alfalfa.

Lupines reach their heights in the western United States because they can stand dry, poor soil. The name *Lupinus* comes from the Latin word for wolf, *lupus*, because the plant was thought to devour the soil. Ironically, lupines, like many others in the family, actually enrich the soil by fixing nitrogen.

The Texas bluebonnet has been called buffalo clover, wolf flower, and *el conejo*, the rabbit, for the white tip on the top petal. Like almost all the peas, the flowers have five petals. One is the "standard," which stands behind or above, the two side petals are the wings, and the two lower ones are joined into the keel, which contains the stamens and pistils.

A Portfolio of Prairie Flowers

Painted by
Michael Eagleton

Sunflower

Helianthus spp.

Prairie clover

Petalostemum spp.

Anemone

Anemone spp.

Plains larkspur

Delphinium virescens

Blue-eyed grass

Sisyrinchium spp.

Blazing star

Mentzelia spp.

Gaillardia

Gaillardia spp.

Poppy mallow

Callirhoë involucrata

Sunflower

Helianthus spp.

For miles on end sunflowers smile gayly at passersby. No other flower more loudly proclaims itself queen of the prairie and plains, always with its face to the sun.

In late summer the unmistakable brilliant yellow flowers cover old fields and follow fencerows, roadsides, and railroad tracks. Some tower over a person.

Their name hails from *helios*, sun, and *anthos*, flower. There are perhaps twenty species of sunflowers, most of which are coarse plants with large leaves. Some are annual, like the common sunflower famous as a cultivated species; others are perennial, like *Helianthus maximiliani*, named for Prince Maximilian, a naturalist who explored the West in the 1830s.

Besides the cheer they bring, sunflowers serve a number of useful purposes. Their seeds feed people and animals; Dakota Indians boiled the flower heads and drank the concoction for lung ailments. Tubers of Jerusalem artichoke, a wide-ranging sunflower, are delicious. And sunflower stalks, along with corncobs and buffalo chips, fueled sodbusters' stoves on the treeless plains.

Prairie clover

Petalostemum spp.

The rosy florets of prairie clover look for all the world like a ballerina's tutu, encircling the tall center cone of the flower head. They belong to a family well known for its economic importance: the bean or pea family.

But prairie clover is a confusion to botanists. Its flowers are not made like those of others in the pea family. Each small flower in the cluster has one heart-shaped petal, called a banner or standard. The other four parts of the flower appear as petals or stamens—hence its genus name, *Petalostemum*, Greek for petal and stamen. Which they truly are remains a question.

Whatever the flower parts, this is a valuable wild legume whose presence indicates healthy grassland. Prairie clover enhances soil and is highly nutritious forage for livestock. Mixed with the bark of white oak, the florets were used as diarrhea medicine. And tea brewed from its roots was administered to people suffering from measles.

During its blooming period, the floral circlet has the interesting habit of moving from the base to the top of the cone.

Anemone

Anemone spp.

Anemone or Wind-floure, is so called, for the floure doth never open it self but when the wind doth blow. . . ," wrote sixteenth-century herbalist John Gerard, quoting Pliny. It has long been stated, though not always accepted, that the name anemone arose from the Greek word for wind, *anemos*. On the prairies and plains, where the wind always blows, this version is easy to accept.

Pasque flower, another common name, is given because it blooms around Easter and sometimes well before. People have also called the anemone crocus, blue tulip, lion's head, gosling, April fool, and American pulsatilla.

To brave early spring in the Plains region a plant needs protection from sudden spring storms. The anemone is clothed all over with silky hairs. As Hal Borland has written of these blue satin beauties: "Of all early wildflowers these are the bravest, not blooming in sheltered woods, but out in the big open . . . where the wind cuts to the bone in late March."

Plains larkspur

Delphinium virescens

The plains or prairie larkspur is a ghostly cousin to the deep blue flowers most often associated with our western brand of larkspur. The sepals give the plains larkspur what color it has, and the petals are inconspicuous. As in all larkspurs, the upper sepal has a spur, but the two upper petals also have spurs that project into the sepal's spur, giving it a "double nature."

On erect stems, sometimes reaching five feet, the plains larkspur is in full bloom by June, before the taller grasses reach full stature. A perennial, it comes in after fires, with prairie phlox and butterfly weed.

This larkspur, as with all others, possesses alkaloids poisonous to cattle.

Delphinium is the Greek word for dolphin, the animal they believed protected seafarers on Mediterranean voyages. The genus name dates back at least to the first century A.D., when the Greek physician Dioscorides used it. Germans called it *Rittersporn*, the Spaniards *espuela de caballero*, the Swedish *riddarspore*, all meaning "knight's spur."

Blue-eyed grass

Sisyrinchium spp.

The flat, sharp-edged, narrow stems and leaves make it readily apparent how this plant came to be called a grass. It is not, however, a grass, but instead belongs to the iris family. "Blue-eyed grass is one of the irises—a most modest iris to be sure," writes John Madson, "but one standing in high favor if not in size."

Examination bears out this relationship. Among iris qualities, are blue-eyed grass's three stamens, folded leaves, and inferior ovary, with the flower divided into six petal-like segments. Each segment ends in a fine point like the nib on a fountain pen. The deep blue to violet flowers of blue-eyed grass are usually less than an inch in size, with yellow centers that may explain another name, "eyebright."

Blue-eyed grass is a prairie original, and with other spring and early summer wildflowers its presence reveals that the land has been treated kindly. Meadows, woods, and moist places are its home.

Blazing star

Mentzelia spp.

The name *Mentzelia* honors the seventeenth-century German botanist, Christian Mentzel, but the common family name for blazing star and its cousins is most telling. This family is called stickleaf—and for good reason. The lance-shaped leaves and the stems of this plant are armed with barbs, bristles, and stinging hairs that attach themselves when touched. Little pagoda-shaped hairs are responsible for the sandpapery texture. Down south in Texas the plant is known curiously as *buena mujer,* "good woman," for its clinging qualities.

Mentzelia is almost entirely native to the Americas, and many species are found in the western United States. They avoid wet environments and especially take to warm and dry places with sandy and gravelly soils, a preference favorable for a prairieland flower.

Blazing star is a real showstopper—with five or ten white or yellow petals and sepals and profuse stamens bunched like a wire brush in the center. Stickleafs stay closed most of the day, opening in late afternoon. They bloom from June or July until September or October.

Gaillardia

Gaillardia spp.

The bright red, pink, and yellow of gaillardia splash themselves across the prairie in the colors of a woven blanket, and several of its names suggest just that—blanketflower, Indian blanket, and firewheel.

Western though it justly seems, the generic name given to it in 1788 honors an amateur French botanist, Gaillard de Charentonneau. Gaillardia displays uniform traits of the enormous and often perplexing composite family, that includes among others asters, daisies, thistles, dandelions, and sunflowers. In composites, the "flower" is actually a number of tiny individual flowers packed tightly together like commuters in a subway car. Composites, wrote Hal Borland, "have their own villages and small cities." Biologically, however, the collection functions as one flower, attracting a host of different insects as pollinators.

The central flowers are called disk flowers, the outer ones ray flowers. Gaillardia's ray flowers, eight or ten of them, are all yellow or often tipped with yellow, and have teeth or lobes at the end. The disk flowers, which form a dome, are purplish-red, brownish, or orange.

Poppy mallow

Callirhoë involucrata

Plants sometimes make strange bedfellows. This prairie beauty is cousin to okra, cotton, hibiscus, and hollyhock. All are in the mallow family, the same one that gives us the marshmallow, that melt-in-your-mouth confection originally made from the sticky sap of the plant's root. One trait that all flowers of the family share is a column of united stamens in the center of the blossom.

Poppy mallow, or wine cups, has five crimson or cherry-red petals with square or notched tips. The petals tend to overlap one another, but flare out at the top of the flower.

The stems crisscross in a sprawling, entangled, low-growing mat, sometimes covering acres with intense color. Poppy mallows prefer sandy or gravelly soils, and flower in spring in the southern Plains and later as one moves north.

Select Bibliography

Ajilvsgi, Geyata. *Wildflowers of Texas.* Shearer Publishing, Bryan, Texas, 1984.

Arnberger, Leslie P. *Flowers of the Southwest Mountains.* Southwest Parks and Monuments Association, Tucson, 1982.

Barr, Claude S. *Jewels of the Plains.* University of Minnesota Press, Minneapolis, 1983.

Borland, Hal. *Sundial of the Seasons.* J.B. Lippincott, Philadelphia, 1964.

Bowen, Ezra. *The High Sierra.* Time-Life Books, 1972.

Craighead, John J., Frank C. Craighead, Jr., and Ray J. Davis. *A Field Guide to Rocky Mountain Wildflowers.* Houghton Mifflin, Boston, 1963.

Dana, Mrs. William Starr. *How to Know the Wild Flowers.* Dover Publications, New York, 1963.

Durant, Mary. *Who Named the Daisy? Who Named the Rose?* Dodd, Mead, New York, 1976.

Eiseley, Loren. *The Immense Journey.* Random House, New York, 1946.

Farb, Peter. *Face of North America.* Harper & Row, New York, 1963.

Fielder, Mildred. *Plant Medicine and Folklore.* Winchester Press, New York, 1975.

Foster, Sylvia. "Chaparral." In *This Good Earth.* Les Line, ed. Crown Publishers, New York, in cooperation with the National Audubon Society, 1974.

Hansen, Harry, ed. *California: A Guide to the Golden State.* Hastings House, New York, 1967.

Haskin, Leslie L. *Wild Flowers of the Pacific Coast.* Dover Publications, New York, 1977.

Heywood, V. H., ed. *Flowering Plants of the World.* Mayflower Books, New York, 1978.

Kelley, Don Greame. *Edge of a Continent: The Pacific Coast from Alaska to Baja.* American West Publishing Co., Palo Alto, 1971.

Kirk, Ruth. *Desert: The American Southwest.* Houghton Mifflin, Boston, 1973.

McGinnies, William G. *Discovering the Desert.* University of Arizona Press, Tucson, 1981.

McNulty, Tim. *Olympic National Park: Where the Mountain Meets the Sea.* Woodlands Press, Del Mar, 1984.

Madson, John. *Where the Sky Began: Land of the Tallgrass Prairie.* Sierra Club Books, San Francisco, 1982; "The Running Country," In *This Good Earth*, Les Line, ed. Crown Publishers in cooperation with National Audubon Society, 1974.

Meeuse, Bastiaan and Sean Morris. *The Sex Life of Flowers.* Facts on File Publications, New York, 1984.

Morgan, Neil. *The Pacific States.* Time-Life Books, New York, 1967.

Munz, Philip A. *California Spring Wildflowers*, 1961; *California Mountain Wildflowers*, 1963; *Shore Wildflowers of California, Oregon and Washington*, 1964. University of California Press, Berkeley.

National Geographic Society. *Our Continent: A Natural History of North America.* The National Geographic Society, Washington, D.C., 1976.

Niering, William A. *The Audubon Society Field Guide to North American Wildflowers, Eastern Region.* Alfred A. Knopf, New York, 1979.

Orr, Richard T. and Margaret C. Orr. *Wildflowers of Western America.* Galahad Books, New York, 1974.

Parsons, Mary Elizabeth. *The Wildflowers of California.* Dover Publications, New York, 1966.

Plowden, David. *Floor of the Sky: The Great Plains.* Sierra Club Books, San Francisco, 1972.

Rickett, Harold William. *Wild Flowers of the United States.* Vols. 3, 4, 5, and 6. New York Botanical Garden and McGraw-Hill, 1966–.

Spellenberg, Richard. *The Audubon Society Field Guide to North American Flowers, Western Region.* Alfred A. Knopf, New York, 1979.

Steinhart, Peter. "As the old oaks fall." *AUDUBON.* September, 1978.

Watts, May Theilgaard. *Reading the Landscape of America.* Macmillan, New York, 1975.

Weber, William A. *Rocky Mountain Flora.* Colorado Associated University Press, Boulder, 1976.

Welsh, Stanley L. *Flowers of the Canyon Country.* Brigham Young University Press, Provo, Utah, 1971.

Williams, Richard L. *The Northwest Coast.* Time-Life Books, New York, 1973.

Zwinger, Ann H. and Beatrice E. Willard. *Land Above the Trees: A Guide to American Alpine Tundra.* Harper & Row, New York, 1972.